T0144967

Copyright © 2021 Sharon Dole & Vincent Bryan.

All rights reserved. No part of this book may be used or reproduced by any means, graphic, electronic, or mechanical, including photocopying, recording, taping or by any information storage retrieval system without the written permission of the author except in the case of brief quotations embodied in critical articles and reviews.

Balboa Press books may be ordered through booksellers or by contacting:

Balboa Press
A Division of Hay House
1663 Liberty Drive
Bloomington, IN 47403
www.balboapress.com
844-682-1282

Because of the dynamic nature of the Internet, any web addresses or links contained in this book may have changed since publication and may no longer be valid. The views expressed in this work are solely those of the author and do not necessarily reflect the views of the publisher, and the publisher hereby disclaims any responsibility for them.

Any people depicted in stock imagery provided by Getty Images are models, and such images are being used for illustrative purposes only.
Certain stock imagery © Getty Images.

ISBN: 979-8-7652-2560-8 (sc)
ISBN: 979-8-7652-2561-5 (e)

Library of Congress Control Number: 2022903601

Print information available on the last page.

Balboa Press rev. date: 03/17/2022

BALBOA.PRESS
A DIVISION OF HAY HOUSE

First Encounter with a Duppy

It was one of those beautiful evenings in Jamaica when the stars light up the sky at sunset. Vincent was in the yard climbing a naseberry tree to pick his favorite fruit when he heard his mother call, "Bwoy, unnu come dung outta di tree and go wid Sistah to de shop fi buy saltfish. Mi waan tuh mek ackee and saltfish fi tomorrow's breakfast."

"Mi a come," responded Vincent. Reluctantly, he climbed down from the tree and set out with his sister Doris for the shop at Baker Crossroads, a mile's walk from their home.

Naseberry trees, also known as sapodillas, can be found throughout the Caribbean. They are very sweet and taste like a combination of cinnamon and pear.

Ackee and saltfish is the national dish of Jamaica and is often served at breakfast. Ackee grows on trees and is, therefore, considered a fruit. However, it is cooked like a vegetable.

When Vincent and Doris reached the gate of their front yard, they saw a tall, strange-looking man walking by. Thinking the man may be Devon, one of their neighbors, the children ran to catch up with him. However, as close as they seemed to get to the man, they were never able to catch up. Although he was only an arm's length in front of them, close enough to hear their voices, the man never turned around to see who was following him.

As the children were approaching the stranger, they could hear his footsteps--tap, tap, tap---on the gravel road. Doris was walking ahead of Vincent and was the first one to notice, "Vincent, unnu si? Di man nuh hab no fut!" Indeed, in the place where the man's feet should be, there was a blank space from his ankles on down which made him look like he was floating on air. At first, they thought it was a trick the man was playing on them. But when they looked up, they noticed that the part of the man's body where his head should be appeared misty, making him unidentifiable.

Still thinking the strange man might be Devon, the children expected him to turn in to the house where Devon lived. Instead, he lifted straight up off the ground and disappeared into thin air.

Leroy, the children's cousin, was standing at Devon's gate waiting for his friend to arrive. When the children asked Leroy if he had seen the strange man, he responded, "Mi neva did si di mon and an awah hav gaan by." Frightened at hearing that their cousin had not seen the strange man, although he had been standing there for an hour, Vincent and Doris hurried on their way.

When they reached Baker Crossroads and related their story of the stranger to the men at the store playing dominoes, the men told the children that they had just seen a duppy, "Lawd a massa, di duppy play a trick pan yuh." The children were not surprised to hear this, as they already knew in their hearts that they had encountered a duppy. As the African proverb goes, "He who feels it, knows it."

On the way back from the shop, the children had to pass by the house of Leila whose front yard was covered in deep foliage. Vincent, observing movement under the foliage, excitedly said to his sister, "Mi a frightened, di duppy mon hides unda di bush."

Leila's watchdog, Busta, was not chained up as he usually was and, as the children approached Leila's gate, he began running towards them, barking ferociously.

In a flash, Busta turned and started running in the opposite direction, barking even more ferociously. The children could not see who or what the dog was chasing but they could hear sounds like it was attacking someone. Suddenly, the strange-looking man who they had seen earlier appeared out of nowhere and both man and dog ran pell-mell into the bush behind the house and disappeared.

18

The children became so frightened that they ran all the way home, Doris losing her shoes in the process.

20

They knew that Doris would be punished if their parents found out that she lost her shoes. So early the next morning, gathering up their courage, the children retraced their steps to see if they could find Doris's shoes. Sure enough, the shoes were in the same place where they had fallen off her feet the night before. The duppy was nowhere to be seen.

About the Authors

Sharon Dole, professor emeritus of education at Western Carolina University, was on a teaching assignment in Mandeville, Jamaica, when she met Vincent Bryan, who was born in Jamaica but had emigrated to England at the age of 18. At the time of their meeting, Vincent was living in Canada and was visiting his childhood homeplace where his parents were buried. Sharon was captivated by Vincent's stories of his childhood in Jamaica. Now married, the couple reside in North Carolina but spend several weeks in Jamaica every year.

Printed in the United States
by Baker & Taylor Publisher Services